THOMAS EDISON
AND HIS 1093 PATENTS

Biography Book Series for Kids

Children's Biography Books

BABY PROFESSOR

EDUCATION KIDS

Speedy Publishing LLC

40 E. Main St. #1156

Newark, DE 19711

www.speedypublishing.com

Copyright 2017

Thomas Edison

In this book, we're going to talk about the inventor Thomas Edison and his 1,093 patents. So, let's get right to it!

WHO WAS THOMAS ALVA EDISON?

Thomas Alva Edison is considered to be one of the greatest inventors the world has ever known. In addition to being a great inventor himself, he knew how to put a team together to collaborate on inventions. He was also an excellent businessman and found ways to make his inventions commercially successful. He became a very wealthy man from his creations.

THOMAS ALVA EDISON

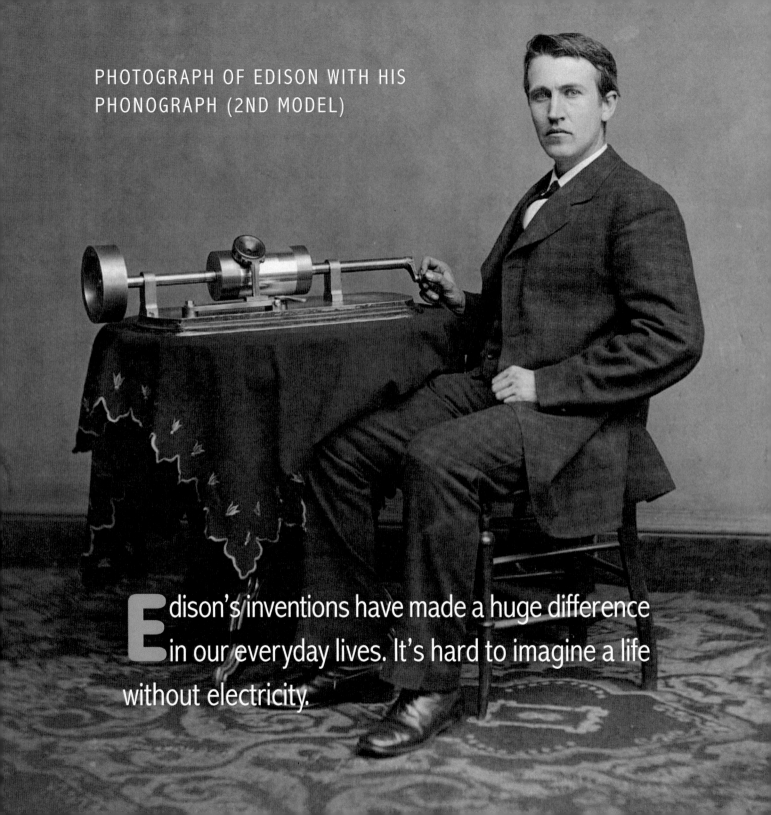

PHOTOGRAPH OF EDISON WITH HIS
PHONOGRAPH (2ND MODEL)

Edison's inventions have made a huge difference in our everyday lives. It's hard to imagine a life without electricity.

When we turn on the lights or our computers or our washing machines, we assume that electricity is going to flow through the wires.

POWER TRANSMISSION LINES

Without the efforts of two brilliant inventors, Thomas Edison and Nikola Tesla, we wouldn't have electricity in our homes today. The first power transmission line wasn't available in the United States until 1889.

YOUNG THOMAS EDISON

EARLY LIFE

Thomas Alva Edison was born in February of 1847. When he reached toddler age, he began to tinker with things and pull them apart to see how they worked. When Edison was in elementary school, he was interested in so many things that his mind wandered. His schoolteacher thought he wasn't very smart because he couldn't focus on his schoolwork.

When Edison's mother found out that his teacher thought he was a dull student, she immediately took him out of school and decided to home school him. She created an entire curriculum designed just for him.

NANCY MATTHEWS ELLIOTT
THOMAS EDISON'S MOTHER

PORT HURON, MICHIGAN

Edison, who was nicknamed "Al" from his middle name of Alva, was an avid reader and science buff. He was always curious about the greater world outside of their neighborhood of Port Huron, Michigan.

When he became a famous inventor, he always talked about how his mother's encouragement made a difference in his life. Without her guidance and approval, he knew he would never have been able to succeed.

EDISON LEARNS HOW TO USE THE TELEGRAPH

When he was only 12 years old, Edison was already running his own business. He offered newspapers and candy for sale on the Grand Trunk railway line that was the connection between Port Huron and Detroit. He ran this business for four years until one day something happened that changed his life.

The young son of the stationmaster ran out on the tracks in front of an oncoming freight train. Edison raced to the boy, grabbed him up off the tracks, and brought him back to his distraught father.

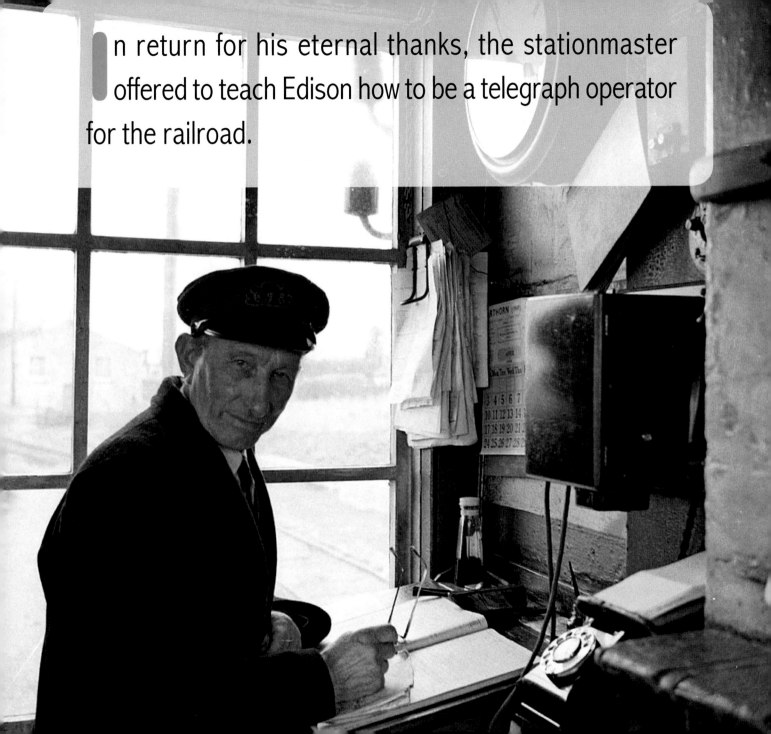

In return for his eternal thanks, the stationmaster offered to teach Edison how to be a telegraph operator for the railroad.

Edison was so excited! In order to become a telegrapher, Edison learned everything possible about how to use electricity. Although he was only 16 at the time, he quickly figured out how batteries operated and how to use them. He also learned how to properly wire circuits and studied the scientific properties of magnets in combination with electricity.

WHAT WAS EDISON'S FIRST INVENTION?

Edison was only 22 years old when he filed his first patent. He was employed as a telegrapher for the railroad, when he came up with the idea for an Electrographic Vote Recorder.

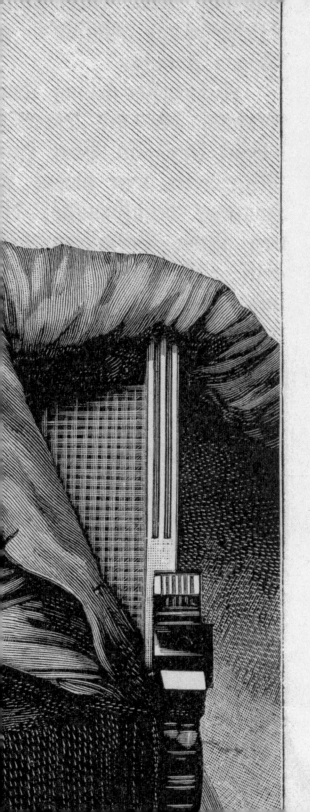

He reasoned that it would help the members of Congress vote more quickly than their traditional voice method. The invention was connected to the desk of a clerk and the names of the members of Congress were embedded in the machine. They would move a switch to vote yes or no and wheels on the device would calculate the results of the vote.

There was only one problem with his machine. Ironically, the members of Congress didn't want to vote faster! So, Edison didn't have a way to sell his machine. Even though he didn't make money on his invention, Edison didn't give up.

THOMAS EDISON AND THE PERFECTED-
PHONOGRAPH-GROUP IN 1888

EDISON STOCK TELEGRAPH TICKER

WHAT WAS EDISON'S FIRST PROFITABLE INVENTION?

Soon, Edison moved to New York. He continued to experiment with new ideas that he had for inventions. He created an improved stock ticker, which he called the Universal stock ticker. His invention allowed all the tickers on the line to print the same information at the same time.

This device allowed financial information to be transmitted much more quickly. Edison sold the rights for his invention to the Gold and Stock Telegraph Company for $40,000.

W ith this huge financial success, Edison was able to quit his day job and become a full-time inventor.

He set up a small laboratory in Newark, New Jersey in 1870 and put some machinists to work. Because he was now independent, he was able to create more telegraphy inventions and sell them for the highest bid. He developed the quadraplex telegraph. This amazing invention was able to send out four signals at a time—two signals in one direction and two signals in the opposite direction—on the same wire!

This invention would increase profits for telegraph companies and decrease costs at the same time. When he invented the machine, the Western Union Telegraph Company was the industry leader.

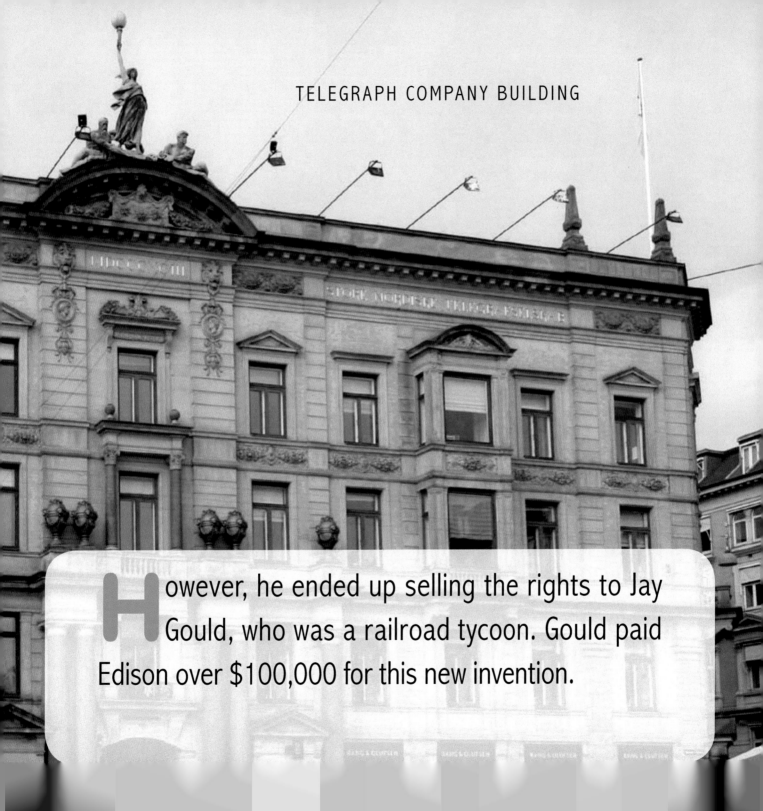

TELEGRAPH COMPANY BUILDING

However, he ended up selling the rights to Jay Gould, who was a railroad tycoon. Gould paid Edison over $100,000 for this new invention.

EDISON CONCERT PHONOGRAPH

WHAT WAS EDISON'S FAVORITE INVENTION?

With this huge amount of money, Edison moved his operation to Menlo Park, New Jersey in 1876. Western Union wanted him to work on a telephone device such as the one that Alexander Graham Bell had invented. Instead, in 1877, Edison invented what was to become his favorite invention—the phonograph.

This invention could do something amazing. It could record someone speaking and play that recording back. The vibration made by the person's voice would make a needle move, which created etchings into a drum that had been wrapped in tin foil. The very first message that was ever recorded was Edison's voice reciting the children's poem, "Mary had a little lamb." It was so exciting when Edison and his team heard the message played back!

PHONOGRAPH

dison had invented the phonograph for letter dictation, but it soon expanded into the entertainment market. By listening to a record of musical instruments or singers accompanied by music,

people could use the phonograph to enjoy a concert in their own homes. Edison, who had been almost deaf since childhood, had given the world the wonderful gift of home music.

HOW LONG DID IT TAKE FOR EDISON AND HIS TEAM TO IMPROVE THE LIGHT BULB?

Many people think that Edison invented the light bulb, but that isn't true. A British inventor obtained a patent the year before Edison filed his patent in the United States. Eventually, Edison bought out that inventor, but before that happened, Edison and his employees began testing different materials.

They wanted to make the incandescent light bulb last longer so it would be more practical for people to use in their homes. They used over 1,600 different materials in more than 3,000 experiments before they found the right material for the filament. By the year 1882, only 3,000 light bulbs had been sold, but a decade later Edison had over 3 million active customers. He also created the entire system of distribution that was needed to bring electricity into people's homes.

EDISON IN HIS LABORATORY

HOW MANY PATENTS DID HE HAVE?

By the time he passed away at the age of 84, Edison had 1,093 United States patents and several hundreds more in other countries. He generally applied for two patents or more every single month.

His inventions improved technologies or created new ones for these categories:

- Batteries
- Electric lights
- Electric power and its distribution
- Telegraphs
- Telephones
- Phonographs and Sound Recordings
- Motion Pictures
- Cement and Mining Industries

EDISON'S FIRST MOVIE MACHINE,
THE KINETOSCOPE

KIA SILVERBROOK

DOES ANY INVENTOR HOLD MORE PATENTS THAN EDISON?

Today there are several different inventors who hold more patents than Edison. Shunpei Yamazaki of Japan and Kia Silverbrook of Australia are currently the top two prolific inventors in the world.

WERE ANY OF EDISON'S INVENTIONS FAILURES?

Every inventor has some inventions that don't measure up or are never commercially successful. Edison tried to invent a way to extract iron from surrounding ore that wasn't usable. He sold all the stock he had in the electric company he founded, General Electric, in order to finance the work needed but he wasn't successful at accomplishing this. He lost all the money he had invested.

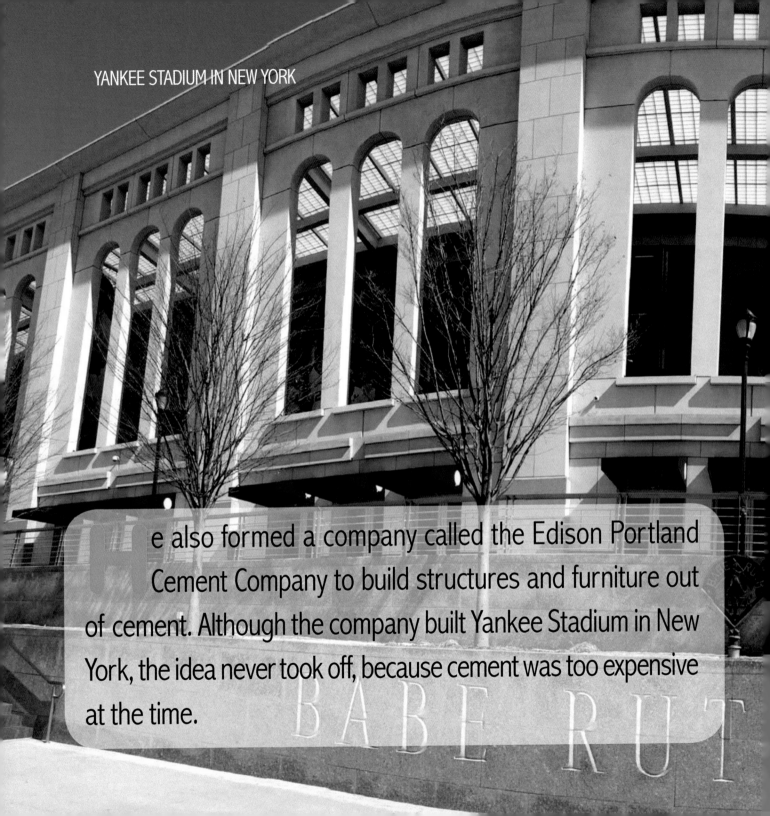

e also formed a company called the Edison Portland Cement Company to build structures and furniture out of cement. Although the company built Yankee Stadium in New York, the idea never took off, because cement was too expensive at the time.

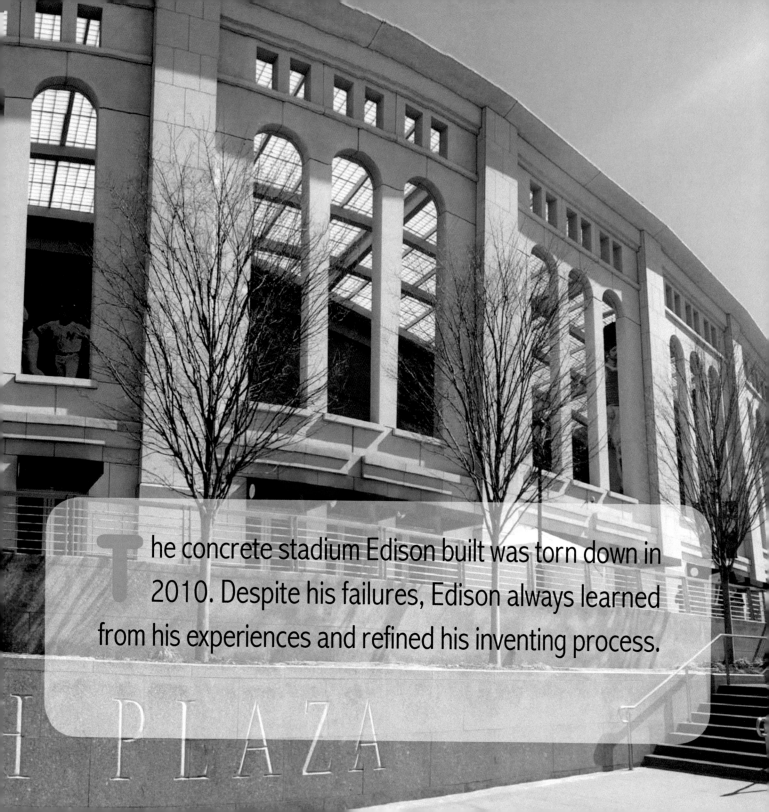

The concrete stadium Edison built was torn down in 2010. Despite his failures, Edison always learned from his experiences and refined his inventing process.

Edison
An Amazing Man

Thomas Alva Edison was one of the most prolific inventors who ever lived. The inventions he created and the process for research and development he established inspire inventors and would-be inventors all over the world.

When there's a will, there's a way.

Awesome! Now that you know more about Thomas Edison you may want to try some electrical experiments on your own using the Baby Professor book You, Too, Can Make Electricity! Experiments for 6th Graders.